CHICAGO PUBLIC LIBRARY

DISCARD

W9-BJK-254

ORIOLE PARK BRANCH
DATE DUE   11-03

DEC 2 0 2003		
JUN 2 5 2004		
DISCARD		

DEMCO 38-296

Oriole Park Branch
7454 W. Balmoral Ave.
Chicago, IL 60656

R03062 06314

Why do we use that?

CHICAGO PUBLIC LIBRARY
ORIOLE PARK BRANCH
5201 N. OKETO   60656

CONTENTS

Franklin Watts
A Division of Grolier Publishing
New York · London · Hong Kong · Sydney
Danbury, Connecticut

Alarm made from a bell in a candle. The bell fell out when the candle melted.

An early alarm using a candle flame to burn through a thread. When the thread broke the weight fell to the floor and made a noise.

In the 1851 Great Exhibition, R. W. Savage exhibited a bed that woke sleepers with a bell, took off the blankets, tilted the mattress, and threw the sleeper on to the floor.

A CLEAN START

This book is all about the things we use and why we use them. Let's start in the bathroom.

Sponge

Soap dissolves the dirt on skin and loosens grease. It was first used by German tribes in the first century A.D. and was made with a mixture of wood ashes and tallow (animal fat).

Real sponges are the skeletons of marine animals called sea sponges. Because they are soft and absorb water they are useful for washing. Nowadays, most sponges are artificial.

Bathtubs help to maintain a person's privacy while he or she is washing. The first known bathtub was used in 1700 B.C. and was from ancient Crete. It looked remarkably like a nineteenth-century tub.

Loofahs are the fiber skeletons of marrow-like plants from North Africa. They are good for scrubbing away dead skin.

Loofah

Olive oil

Strigils

Before soap was invented, the Romans cleaned themselves with olive oil. This, along with the dirt from their bodies, was scraped off using a strigil, or curved scraper.

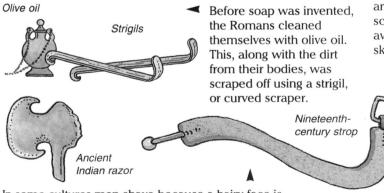

Ancient Indian razor

Nineteenth-century strop

In some cultures men shave because a hairy face is considered dirty or old-looking. Other cultures value beards as a sign of age and wisdom. Shaving was originally done with a special blade which was sharpened, or stropped, using a leather strop. Scalp hair was singed off with red-hot iron or coal, or it was plucked out by hand.

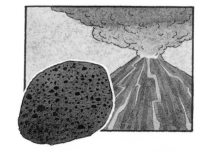

Pumice is volcanic rock that is naturally very rough. It is useful for scraping off ingrained dirt and dead skin.

If bits of food are left in the mouth, tooth enamel is likely to rot. In the past, people ate less sweet food than people do nowadays. Nevertheless, they needed to keep their teeth clean. The modern toothbrush was invented in 1780 by William Addis.

Jar of tooth powder

Some other ways to clean your teeth.

Use a toothpick.

Chew a twig.

Rub them with a cloth.

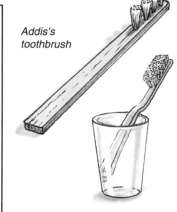

Addis's toothbrush

Betel nut

Toothpaste was once made from ingredients such as powdered horn, pumice stone, and charcoal. Nowadays one of the main ingredients is china clay. The tiny particles in toothpaste work in the same way as sandpaper, rubbing away the dirt from the teeth.

In India, people chew on betel nuts wrapped in pepper-vine leaves flavored with lime. Chewing on betel nuts stimulates blood flow in the gums and hardens the teeth – though it also stains them black.

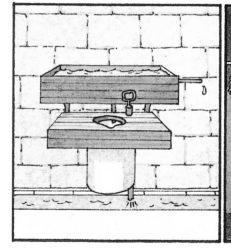

The first flush toilet was invented by Sir John Harington in 1596. One was installed in Richmond Palace for Queen Elizabeth I of England.

Garderobes were toilets built into the thick walls of castles and manor houses. They drained into the moat. Coats were kept in the garderobe because the ammonia from the urine kept away the larvae of moths, which feed on cloth fibers.

Until the late nineteenth century most people in England only had one toilet located at the end of their garden. They used a chamber pot during the night. Some people had a cesspit in the cellar.

Indian villagers often use a special area of woodland as a toilet. This practice is quite sanitary because the hot sun dries out the waste quickly.

In ancient Rome, buckets of salty water holding sponges on sticks were left in the public toilets — for communal use.

An astronaut has to keep a space suit on when spacewalking. If he or she wants to go to the toilet, the urine is collected in a special bag and recycled as water to cool the suit.

3

POTS AND PANS AND USEFUL CANS

Cooking destroys some vitamins, especially those in fruits and vegetables. Because of this, some people choose to eat only raw food. But cooking also destroys dangerous bacteria and softens tough food. We could not easily eat grains like wheat and rice without cooking them. So on balance, cooking does more good than harm. Besides, cooked food tastes good, which is the main reason why so many different foods and cooking equipment have been invented.

▲ One of the earliest examples of fires used for cooking comes from a cave in China where a 500,000-year-old hearth has been found.

Cattle dung is often used for fuel where firewood is in short supply. The dung is made into slabs that burn very slowly, providing a steady cooking temperature.

The first crude gas range was introduced in 1812. Later, special burner rings were devised which, by allowing more air to mix with the gas, burned the gas more efficiently. The Regulo oven thermostat was introduced on gas ranges in 1923 to regulate temperatures.

Over the centuries many women ▲ have been killed while they cooked over open fires because their clothes caught fire. This was called "hearth death."

Clay ovens called tandoors are used in some areas of India. The sides of the tandoor are used for cooking flat bread, known as naan, while meat is roasted over the fire. This arrangement saves on scarce fuel.

The invention of the iron range changed cooking dramatically. Among other things it reduced the number of hearth deaths. The Aga range is a modern version of the iron range but one that conserves fuel. It was invented in 1924 by a blind Swedish scientist, Gustav Dalen. The Aga originally ran on solid fuel but is now heated by gas, oil, or electricity.

Ovens and radar may not seem to be related, but the microwave oven was developed from World War II radar technology. Microwaves make water molecules in the food vibrate and this makes the food become hot. Microwave ovens can cook food very quickly.

If food is cooked properly and sealed in a sterile container, it keeps for a very long time. At first, food was preserved in this way in bottles. Tin cans came into use in 1810, to preserve food for soldiers and sailors while they were away on long assignments. However, the food was often badly cooked and contained live bacteria that caused food poisoning. Cans were originally opened using a hammer and chisel. The first openers were developed around 1855, but more sophisticated rotary ones were invented in the 1930s. Nowadays there are electric can openers, which are especially useful for ill or elderly people. ▶

"Bull's head" can opener, 1885

Cans of beef left by Robert Falcon Scott's Antarctic expedition of 1912 were still edible decades later.

Freezing reduces the activity of the microbes that make food decay. Prepacked frozen food became popular thanks to the efforts of the American businessman and inventor Clarence Birdseye. He saw how fish caught by Inuit on the Labrador coast froze as soon as they were landed – and were still fresh months later. Birdseye copied the idea when he returned home, patenting a process of fast freezing in 1925. It took a while to become popular, but now people in the U.S. consume several million tons of convenient, hygienic frozen food each year.

Bakelite jug, 1932

Plastic is often used for kitchen surfaces and utensils. It is light and waterproof. However, the first plastics were soft and melted easily. The first tough, heat-resistant plastic was introduced in 1909 by Dr. Leo Hendrik Baekeland. He called it Bakelite.

Before dishwashing liquid was introduced, people used ashes, sand, or brick dust to clean dishes. Scots used heather to scour pots clean.

Nowadays, detergents make washing dishes a lot easier. Detergents work by reducing the surface tension of water. The oil particles break up and the dirt is held in suspension. The first detergent, called Nekal, was made in 1917. ▶

Fingers are very useful for handling food, but they're blunt and they get sticky and dirty. Knives were the first pieces of cutlery to be used, and were a great improvement on human teeth for cutting large chunks of food. The first crude stone knives were made perhaps three million years ago. They were followed much later by spoons and then by forks.

FOOD...

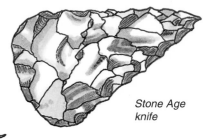

Stone Age knife

Ancient Turkish fork

Roman spoon

Some Stone Age wooden forks may date from as long ago as 7000 B.C. They were two-pronged, which would have made it difficult to skewer small objects. It's thought that they were used to hold down meat while cutting it, in the same way that a carving fork is used nowadays. Modern dining forks originated in Italy, and were brought to England in the seventeenth century by Thomas Coryat.

Medieval knife

Knives used to be very pointed, and were used to cut and then spear the food. In the Middle Ages it was customary to bring your own knife to a meal.

In the Middle Ages, people didn't use plates but instead ate from a large slice of bread or a wooden platter called a trencher. A trencherman is someone who likes to eat a lot of food.

In South Indian food halls, food is served on fresh banana leaves, which are cheap, readily available, and are thrown away after use.

Chopsticks are used throughout the Far East. They originated in China during the Shang dynasty (c.1600–1028 B.C.). In China, chopsticks were considered superior to knives because they were used by scholars. Scholars were more highly thought of than warriors who carried knives.

Chopsticks can be made from ivory, wood, bamboo, or plastic. In general, the chopsticks of China are longer and more blunt than those of Japan, which are usually tapered. The Japanese tend to use disposable wooden chopsticks, throwing away about twenty billion of them each year.

AND DRINK

Tea bags were the idea of an American tea salesman who first tried putting samples of tea into silk bags in the 1920s. Odorless and tasteless paper is now used. The big advantage of tea bags is that there are no messy leaves to wash out of the teapot.

Many Russians use a samovar for making tea. A central tube is filled with hot charcoal and this tube heats the surrounding water, which brews the tea in a pot on top. The teapot is refilled from the hot water.

Aluminum is not normally used for teapots because it turns the tea black.

In seventeenth-century England, people would pour their tea from the cup into the saucer to cool it before drinking it. This practice changed gradually and the saucer now goes under the cup to catch spilled liquid. Drinking from the saucer is thought to be rude.

Straws have been used since very ancient times when the hollow stems of plants were used. From the late nineteenth century, straws were made from waxed paper, but they are now usually made from plastic.

Corkscrews are used for pulling corks from bottles without breaking up the cork. The earliest descriptions date from Tudor times, but the Reverend Samuel Henshaw devised the easy-to-use, double-thread corkscrew in 1795.

Liquid chocolate was originally a bitter drink made from cocoa beans and spices sacred to the Aztecs of Mexico. They called it *chocolatl*. The court of Montezuma II, the Aztec emperor, is said to have drunk fifty jars a day! The *conquistador* Hernan Cortés introduced cocoa beans to Europe in the 1520s, where the drink later became a popular addition to coffeehouse menus as an aid to sleep and digestion. Cocoa beans are now more often used to produce solid chocolate bars and sweets.

Cocoa beans

Clay cart

Wooden dollhouse

Pottery donkey

Chalk snobs – small cubes for throwing and scooping up

Wooden diabolo

Bone flute

Most early toys were made from clay, bone, metal, and wood.

TOYS...

All over the world children play with toys and games. Play teaches us to use our imaginations, think logically, and move quickly. As in life, there are rules to follow, and penalties to be paid if they're broken.

Early dolls made from wood, wax, china, and rags.

Teddy bears were invented after President Theodore "Teddie" Roosevelt refused to kill a bear cub when out hunting. In 1902 a shop owner named Morris Michtom saw a cartoon of this episode in a newspaper, and asked if he could make a small bear and name it "Teddy's Bear." Cuddly teddy bears were soon being produced and sold by the thousands. The early toys looked more like real bears than later versions.

Spinning tops were known in ancient Greece and the Far East. They became popular in Europe in the fourteenth century. By the nineteenth century there were professional top spinners who could make tops jump steps or "walk" up a slope.

AND GAMES

Early dice were originally fashioned from sheeps' ankle bones and had only four numbered sides. Later, the Romans used dice with six numbered sides, which they called *tesserae*. *Tesserae* were made of bone, ivory, or a stone called onyx. They rolled easily and came to rest with one face clearly facing upward so that they could determine results in games of chance.

Greek marble

Modern glass marble

Marbles were played by ancient Greeks, Romans, and Egyptians. In Greece real marble spheres were used. The game of marbles is a child's version of bowls, and in some parts of Scotland the game is still called "bools."

Twelfth-century chess knight

The earliest chess pieces may date from the second century A.D. Known as the war game *chaturanga,* chess was certainly played in seventh-century India. *Chaturanga* had four types of pieces, including the horse, which developed into the knight, and the chariot, which became the castle. ►

Some Tarot cards

The first playing cards used in Europe were a set of twenty-two, called the Tarot. The Tarot were picture cards. Gambling games could be played with them, and they were also used for fortune telling. They were later combined with a set of fifty-six suited and numbered cards, which arrived in Europe from the East around A.D.1300, to create a pack of seventy-eight cards. Later, the French reduced the number to fifty-two, and the Tarot deck split off to be used only for fortune-telling.

A seventeenth-century French playing card

Ching, Chang, Pok!

Here's a game you can play without any special equipment – the ancient Eastern game known as Ching, Chang, Pok (also called Scissors, Paper, Rock). At the count of three, two players hold out one hand each and make a symbol at the same time. The skill is deciding what hand symbol your opponent will show next. There is no score if both players show the same symbol. Keep playing until one player reaches an agreed number of wins.

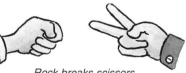

Rock breaks scissors (rock wins).

Scissors cut paper (scissors win).

Paper wraps stone (paper wins).

Casinos use fixed-value gaming chips on roulette tables. This eliminates handling lots of cash, giving change, and checking for forgeries.

ON THE STREET

City streets are full of signs, lights, and other devices. All these things have, or have had, a purpose.

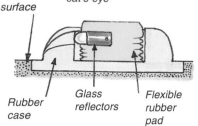

Road surface

Side view of cat's-eye

Rubber case

Glass reflectors

Flexible rubber pad

Cat's-eyes were patented by Percy Shaw in 1934. They consist of a prism reflector mounted in a rubber pad. The prism reflects the light from car headlights. They were especially useful during World War II when there was a blackout in Britain and cars traveled with dimmed headlights so that enemy bombers could not see them.

Fire hydrants and standpipes supply water for fighting fires. In America fire hydrants are above ground. English hydrants are under the street surface. Signs direct English firefighters toward the nearest hydrant.

Public telephones came into use in 1922.

British telephone booth, 1936

When cars were scarce, people could park anywhere — as they do today in small villages. But as cars multiplied it became necessary to control where they parked, and local councils saw an opportunity to make money. Parking meters originated in the US, invented in 1932 by Carlton C. Magee.

Manhole covers are iron or steel inspection hatches for gas, electricity, telephone, water, and sewerage utilities. The covers are rough to prevent people from slipping on them, and they are lifted using a special key. You can often read the name of the maker and even the date on them. Sometimes a sign is placed on a wall opposite a manhole cover as a guide to its position.

In the past people had to use their own torches or lanterns to light their way. The first gas-powered street lighting was demonstrated in London in 1807. Each lamp was lit by hand every evening. Lamplighters later carried a flame on a pole. At the bottom of most modern electrically powered lampposts there is a small panel. Inside there is a junction box connecting the lamp with electric cables under the street.

French street toilet

There have been public lavatories since ancient times. Until private lavatories started to be installed in houses, most ordinary households used communal neighborhood lavatories. In the nineteenth century, sewerage systems were introduced for public health reasons. It cost a penny to use public conveniences in Britain, and many people still "spend a penny" even in their own homes.

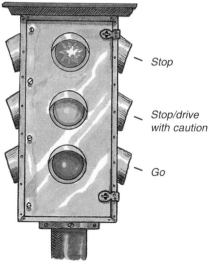

Drains were used in India (2500 B.C.) and Crete (1500 B.C.) to carry away rainwater and sewage. Without drains, rainwater causes temporary flooding. Since bicycles became widely used, the metal gratings across drain covers have usually been placed at right-angles to the street, so that narrow wheels don't get stuck in them.

J. P. Knight, a British railroad signaling engineer, invented a system of red and green gaslights with semaphore arms to direct horse-drawn traffic outside the Houses of Parliament. They were installed around 1868. Unfortunately, a light exploded and killed the policeman operating it.

- Stop
- Stop/drive with caution
- Go

The first electric traffic lights were set up in Cleveland, Ohio, in 1914. They had only red and green lights. The three-color system was introduced in New York in 1918, where it was operated by hand from a "crow's nest" (like the ones used on old sailing ships) in the middle of the street. The first automatic traffic lights followed, in London, in 1925.

Modern direction signs are written in large letters so that drivers can read them as they approach them. Old signposts pointed toward the next town and could be read only as a vehicle passed, which meant that drivers had to slow down in order to read them. Life without signs would be very inconvenient. During World War II, signposts in Britain were removed to confuse possible enemy invaders.

Shop signs were once pictures or large models of objects, rather than names because most people could not read.

Tailor

Pawnbroker

Chemist

Money is a means of exchange between merchants or customers that is more convenient than bartering. The Lydians of Asia Minor are said to have introduced metal coinage around 700 B.C. Paper money was invented by the Chinese around fourteen hundred years ago.

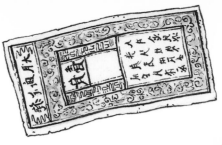

On Pacific islands people used cowrie shells as money.

Lydian coin

Coins in China in the fourth and third centuries B.C. were perforated with a square hole so that they could be hung on a string for safekeeping.

Hard slabs of compressed tea were used as currency in Tibet.

GONE SHOPPING

Shops are as old as civilization. Even in ancient times they had an open front to display the goods, and perhaps a counter. Shopkeepers would often work in their shops manufacturing goods to sell. Shop originally meant "workshop." Early shops specialized in one or two commodities and whole streets would be set aside for a particular trade. There is evidence of this in most old towns from street names such as Butcher Row or Smith Street.

The cash register was invented in Ohio, in 1879 by James Ritty. Cash registers record sales, add up prices, and protect money already collected. Modern versions can read bar codes that give information directly to the cash register without any need to type it in.

Old cash register

The writer A. P. Herbert once presented a check written on a cow!

In Britain, a legal check can be written on anything. A check is an instruction to your bank to pay money to someone from your account. Checks and credit cards are safer and more convenient than carrying around large amounts of cash.

Some dollar bills contain a silver security strip; this and other features make bills difficult to forge.

THE UNITED STATES OF AMERICA
ONE DOLLAR

A unique serial number on each half of the note

Complicated pictures, with lots of tiny lines that are hard to copy

Specially made paper, with areas made extra thin, called water marks

A short history of one-stop shopping

Shopping malls, or shopping centers, combine many shops under one roof. The first shopping mall was built by Sir Thomas Gresham in London in 1568.

Department stores sell many different types of goods under one roof. The first department store was built in Paris in 1850.

Supermarkets are self-service stores that sell a wide range of groceries. The first supermarket was opened by Michael Cullen in 1930 in Jamaica, New York.

Not everyone likes shopping. It's time-consuming and hard work if you have to visit a lot of stores to find the things you need. Putting different stores under one roof is a great help but getting the items home has always been a problem.

Old shopping cart

Handling sugar infested with certain mites can cause a skin inflamation called grocer's itch.

Price tags were first widely used in the eighteenth century to avoid haggling. Aristocratic French refugees who fled to England after the French Revolution were amazed to see that even wandering butchers and grocers would stick labels on all the various goods on their trays. In addition to price tags, stores now attach security tags to packages to make it more difficult to steal them.

Shopping baskets on wheels (shopping trolleys) were introduced in 1936 by S. N. Goldman of Standard Humpty Dumpty Food Markets. His business boomed as people piled goods onto their carts knowing that they would not have to carry heavy bags around the store.

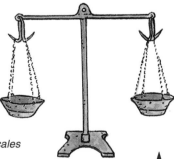

Roman scales

In many countries, goods may be wrapped by the shopkeeper in plain paper or even in large leaves. Prepackaging is a recent development that keeps goods fresh and clean, saves time in the store, and allows the producer to describe and advertise the product, but also produces a lot of waste.

Weighing is often the easiest way to assess the volume or quantity of goods, and weighing scales have been used for thousands of years. Modern electronic scales are very accurate. Goods can be weighed, and the price and weight are automatically registered at the cash register.

SCHOOL SUPPLIES

Children have been going to school for thousands of years, and it's never been very popular with them. But the schools of today are very different from those of the past and so are the things that are used in the classroom.

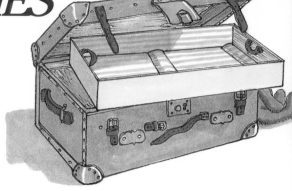

For centuries children sent to boarding school have used large school trunks. They might stay at school right through each term so they needed plenty of clothes and other items. ▼

The blackboard came into existence in the early nineteenth century when a Scottish teacher had the idea of writing on a black painted board with a white chalk. To make colored chalk he mixed ground chalk with coloring and used porridge to bind them together.

▲ Old-fashioned desks had lift-up lids for storing equipment and books inside them, and ink wells into which pens were dipped. The seat was often attached to the desk, or there might be several desks attached together with a bench seat.

The whiteboard is a recent development. Special marker pens are used on a white surface. The board is cleaned with a damp cloth so there's no chalk dust, and no more banging out chalky board erasers against the edge of a blackboard. ►

Felt marker pen

Paper has only recently become cheap enough to use in large quantities in the classroom. For hundreds of years, children used slates to write on instead of paper. Slates can be reused by rubbing out the previous work. They are still used in some countries round the world.

Roman and medieval children used wax tablets made with a layer of wax on a wooden base. Writing was done with a stylus – a stick of reed or metal, sharp at one end for writing and flat at the other end so that the wax could be smoothed out and reused.

Inkwell

Dip pens were used in schools until the 1960s. They leaked, and many schoolchildren had blue, inky fingers for most of the time.

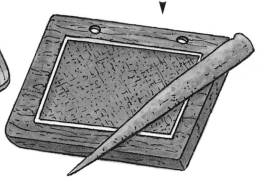

"Lead" pencil

Early pencils were made from a piece of lead encased in wood. In 1795 Nicholas-Jacques Conté produced pencils made from graphite that had been ground, formed into sticks, and baked in a kiln. The graphite in pencils is still called "lead."

Eraser

The first rubber erasers were sold in 1770 by an English maker of mathematical instruments named Mr. Nairne. They were called rubbers because they can rub out pencil marks — rubber is named after erasers, and not the other way around! Natural rubber is a milky liquid, tapped from trees, that hardens in the open air. A similar material produced from dandelions was used in Britain during the rubber shortage in World War II.

Modern fountain pen

Joseph Bramah patented the fountain pen in 1809. It allowed people to write without constantly having to dip their pen in a bottle of ink. Unfortunately, the too-thick ink kept blocking up the pen.

In 1884, a capillary feed mechanism was developed by Lewis E. Waterman. A lever mechanism sucked smooth ink into a rubber sac. Nowadays many fountain pens contain a plastic ink cartridge that can be replaced when empty.

The Biro ballpoint pen

The first ballpoint pen was invented by an American, John Loud, in 1888. An improved version was invented in 1938 by two Hungarian brothers: Lazlo and Georg Biro. The ball at the point of the pen rotates, bringing the ink from the tube to the paper. Franz Seech later developed a special-formula ink that dried instantly on contact with air, preventing smudges. Biros could write under water and they did not leak at high altitudes or low atmospheric pressures. Biros became the standard pens issued to soldiers of the U.S. Army during World War II.

GARDENING GADGETS

People were originally gatherers of wild fruits, cereals, and vegetables. Later they became skilled at cultivating their own plants, and became farmers. At a very early date, plants were no doubt planted with an eye to their beauty as well as their food value. One of the Seven Wonders of the ancient world was the Hanging Gardens of Babylon. Built by King Nebuchadnezzar II in about 600 B.C. in honor of his queen, Amyitis, the gardens of trees, vines, shrubs, and flowers were planted on a huge stepped pyramid 166 feet high.

The wheelbarrow was originally a Chinese military device. It first appeared in Europe in the twelfth century and has been used ever since. The wheelbarrow has only one wheel and so can be turned in a very small area and wheeled along narrow paths. A wheelbarrow is actually a form of lever that makes carrying heavy weights such as soil easier.

The cold frame was probably a sixteenth-century Dutch invention and was used to protect young plants and make them grow quickly without artificial heating. Cold frames are actually warm frames!

16

The lawn as we know it is an English invention dating from the early eighteenth century. Scythes and shears were used to cut the grass, but they could not cut it very short. Lawns with short grass were not a practical proposition until the first cylinder mower was patented by Edwin Budding in 1830. He got the idea from a factory machine that trimmed the pile on cloth. The first large models were pulled by a pony or horse wearing special leather shoes to prevent the animal's hooves from damaging the turf.

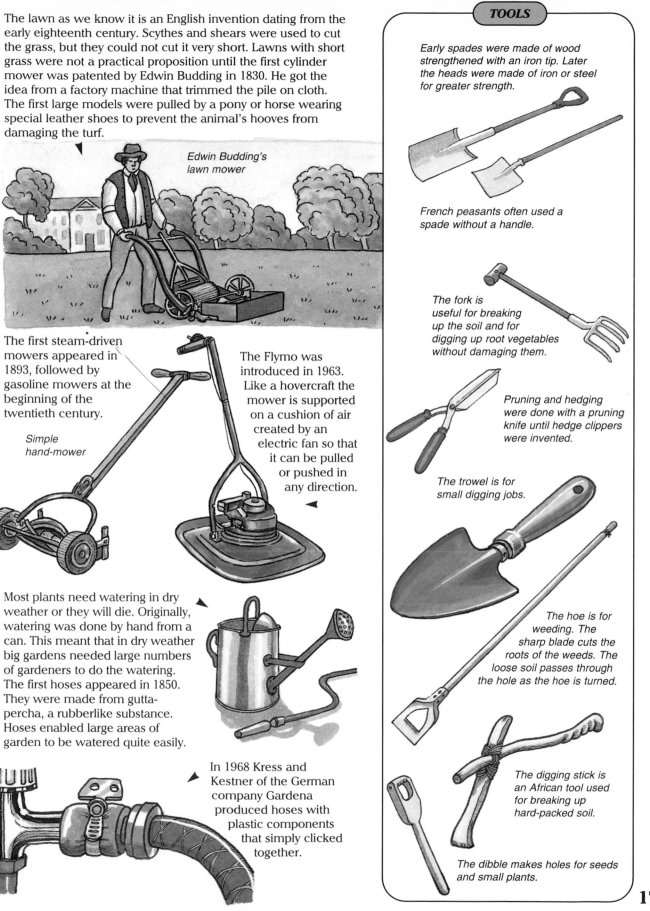

Edwin Budding's lawn mower

The first steam-driven mowers appeared in 1893, followed by gasoline mowers at the beginning of the twentieth century.

Simple hand-mower

The Flymo was introduced in 1963. Like a hovercraft the mower is supported on a cushion of air created by an electric fan so that it can be pulled or pushed in any direction.

Most plants need watering in dry weather or they will die. Originally, watering was done by hand from a can. This meant that in dry weather big gardens needed large numbers of gardeners to do the watering. The first hoses appeared in 1850. They were made from gutta-percha, a rubberlike substance. Hoses enabled large areas of garden to be watered quite easily.

In 1968 Kress and Kestner of the German company Gardena produced hoses with plastic components that simply clicked together.

TOOLS

Early spades were made of wood strengthened with an iron tip. Later the heads were made of iron or steel for greater strength.

French peasants often used a spade without a handle.

The fork is useful for breaking up the soil and for digging up root vegetables without damaging them.

Pruning and hedging were done with a pruning knife until hedge clippers were invented.

The trowel is for small digging jobs.

The hoe is for weeding. The sharp blade cuts the roots of the weeds. The loose soil passes through the hole as the hoe is turned.

The digging stick is an African tool used for breaking up hard-packed soil.

The dibble makes holes for seeds and small plants.

Many sports developed from real fighting techniques . . .

Archery bows evolved from medieval long-bows.

Fencing is a bloodless form of sword fighting.

Javelins are standardized spears.

SPORT

Some sports have an ancient origin, and so does some sports equipment. Balls were used in sport by the ancient Egyptians, and were probably made of blown-up pigs' bladders or other inflated parts of an animal. Bladders were used in footballs until quite recently when modern materials were developed.

The dimensions of a soccer ball were first set by the British Football Association in the nineteenth century. Until recently soccer balls were made of leather, becoming very heavy and water-logged on a muddy playing field. The modern plastic coating keeps them dry.

Cutaway showing inflatable bladder

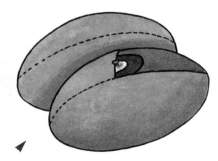

The balls used in American football and Rugby football are egg-shaped so that they can be thrown accurately. This shape also makes it difficult to dribble the ball along the ground.

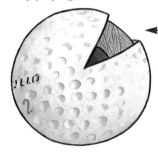

A golf ball is covered with tiny dimples. Air flowing past these dimples helps to make the ball fly further and straighter than if it were smooth. Seventeenth-century golf balls were filled with feathers, but now golf balls contain a variety of synthetic elastic materials.

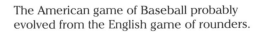

The American game of Baseball probably evolved from the English game of rounders.

Polo, which is like hockey on horseback, developed as a training for war. The game may have been invented by the Persians in the first century A.D. Polo sticks have a long flexible haft and are light enough to be wielded with one hand.

Buzkashi is a game like polo, played in Afghanistan. Games may involve a thousand horsemen. Instead of a ball, players throw or bash the body of a dead goat around to score goals. In one version a flat goat is used . . .

Croquet probably developed from the French game of *paille-maille* in the Middle Ages. Balls are hit between hoops on a lawn. The haft of a croquet mallet is shorter than a polo stick and the head is heavier.

. . . and in another version the goat is inflated.

The name of cricket may come from its bat, or perhaps from its wicket: *creag'et* is Anglo-Saxon for "staff" or "stick." Nowadays the hitting part of the bat is made from willow, which is a very springy wood.

Kites probably originated in China around 1000 B.C. Some were large enough to carry a man and were used for war. In Japan and Thailand, kite fighting between large "male" kites and smaller but more agile "female" ones is very popular. Kite strings coated with ground glass or broken porcelain are used to cut the opponent's line. ►

Lacrosse began as a Native American game, originally called *baggataway*. It was played with as many as a thousand players. Players fought to carry the ball with small nets mounted on wooden sticks. It was a violent game, often played by more than two sets of opponents at a time.

GETTING COMFY

Many early civilizations had no furniture to speak of, and very few home comforts of any kind. Nowadays, the homes of tribal peoples are still often simple, but home has become a place of increasing luxury and comfort for people in many areas. Fixtures like carpets and central heating or cooling systems are now standard.

Carpets were known in Persia in the fifth century B.C. They were one of the luxuries brought back to Europe by the Crusaders, who had seen them spread out on the sand in the tents of desert tribesmen as well as on the floors of rich Arab homes. They were a luxury item in Europe until modern production techniques made them cheaper. Even wall-to-wall carpet is now common. They help to insulate houses as well as providing comfortable floors.

People in Medieval Europe used rushes or straw as floor coverings. It was once illegal in England to throw away rushes, which, because they soaked up urine and other wastes, could be used to make gunpowder. The urine provided saltpeter and the rushes provided sulfur and carbon.

In the Middle East, cushions and simple mattresses are still used instead of furniture in traditional homes.

In the Middle Ages most people had to make do with stools and benches. Chairs with backs were for important people. So little furniture was available that kings would carry it with them from palace to palace. This was still the custom in the sixteenth century. ▶

Steamed furniture appeared around 1850. Wood is heated in a steam box until it becomes flexible; then it's bent and clamped. When dried it retains its new shape. ▼

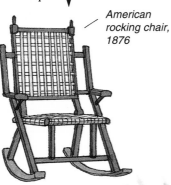

American rocking chair, 1876

◀ Until the sixteenth century, the only form of soft padding was cushions scattered on wooden furniture. Later, horse hair padding, covered in carpet material or velvet, was attached to some expensive furniture. Internal springs were added only in the 1920s.

People in India traditionally relied on small windows and thick walls to keep out the heat of the sun, or on devices such as tatties. Tatties are mats made of the roots of cuscus grass that are soaked with water and hung outside windows. The room is cooled as the water evaporates. ▼

Indian house with tatties

To clean a dusty silk carpet in the desert it is turned over and the dust and dirt are shaken into the sand by people walking on the other side. ▶

Air-conditioning makes houses a lot more comfortable in warm, moist climates. The idea started in America where Willis H. Carrier experimented by passing air through an evaporation chamber. ▶

With a central heating system, one fire heats many rooms. This gives an even, comfortable warmth and means fewer fires or boilers to tend. The Romans had underfloor central heating systems known as hypocausts. ▼

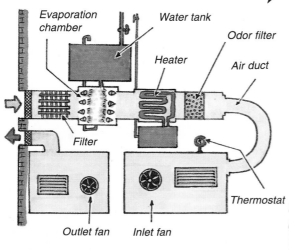

Evaporation chamber
Water tank
Odor filter
Heater
Air duct
Filter
Thermostat
Outlet fan
Inlet fan

Simplified air-conditioning unit

Roman hypocaust

HOME ENTERTAINMENT

In the days before television, many people were able to play musical instruments. Standing beside the River Thames at the time of the Great Fire of London in 1666, Samuel Pepys noted that one refugee boat in three had a pair of virginals in it. A virginal was a popular instrument like a small piano. ►

In the past, people made their own entertainment by playing games or making music, or they told stories about wars and romances, or the adventures of gods and legendary heroes. Home entertainment has changed a lot since then. With the invention of electronic entertainment systems, there are still plenty of games to play and music to make, but nowadays, people watch more and do less.

The first TV picture ever transmitted

The first public demonstration of television was made in 1926 by John Logie Baird. In early transmissions people saw the picture without sound and then the sound without the picture. It was not possible to broadcast sound and pictures at the same time.

Germany transmitted the first regular, filmed TV broadcast in 1935. The broadcast of the Olympic games in 1936 is said to be the first television show with a signal powerful enough to leave the Earth's atmosphere.

The first color TV transmissions were made in the US in 1940 by the Columbia Broadcasting System (CBS).

In the past people tended to go to bed quite soon after darkness fell. When home lighting improved in the nineteenth century, this change, together with cheaper books and with the start of public libraries, helped to make reading a very popular activity.

Movie camera, 1920

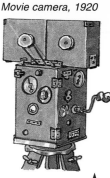

Radio, 1930

History used to be recorded only by books and storytellers. These days history is more often recorded on film or video.

Radio was originally called "wireless" because it needed no wires to carry messages, unlike the telephone or telegraph. We still use radios because we can listen while doing something else.

Record record

Thomas Alva Edison built the first phonograph in 1877. The first recording was the nursery rhyme "Mary Had a Little Lamb," made on a tin-foil cylinder.

Emile Berliner demonstrated the first flat record disc in 1888.

Stereo sound was first demonstrated in 1881. The first stereo disc was patented in 1930. The film Fantasia *had the first stereo sound track.*

Compact discs were introduced in the 1980s. CDs are popular because they are more durable than earlier vinyl records.

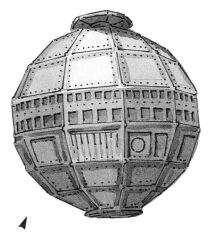

Artificial satellites reflect radio and television signals around the world. The first commercial communications satellite was called *Telstar*, it was launched in 1962.

The coronation of Queen Elizabeth II in 1953 was the first major international broadcast. It was seen in France, West Germany, and the Netherlands.

Video recorders were introduced in 1956 by the Ampex company. These huge machines processed 16 kilometers of tape per hour.

The first flat TV screen was developed by Matsushita in 1979. In the future, wafer-thin televisions may be hung on a wall.

L A M P S

Shetland Islanders used oily seabirds called storm petrels to light their way. With a wick down their throat, these dead birds made excellent lamps.

During World War I, soldiers burned oil in sardine cans for light.

Native Americans used a dead oily "candle fish" inserted in a cleft stick as a lamp.

LIGHTING-UP TIME

Nowadays, it's so easy to flick a switch and light up a room that it's hard to imagine what life was like before electric light was invented. People used candles and lamps, but the light was very dim so they went to bed early and got up early. In the sixteenth century, a curfew starting at nine o'clock in the evening was normal in many towns. During the curfew everyone had to be indoors. The work day might start as early as four o'clock the next morning.

Tudor watchman

Limelight was used to light theater stages from the eighteenth to the late nineteenth centuries. If lime (calcium oxide) is heated to a very high temperature, it glows brilliantly white. At first the lime was heated by gas, then later by electrically powered carbon arcs.

Sir Humphrey Davy invented the electric arc lamp in 1808 but this invention had to wait for suitable electric generators before it could be used for street lighting. The light it produces is so strong that it cannot be used for domestic lighting. Instead people use arc lamps for floodlighting, for large film projectors, and for searchlights.

◄ The first practical electric light bulb was devised by Thomas Alva Edison in 1879. Instead of the modern tungsten filament, Edison used a scorched cotton thread.

Whales used to be a major source of lamp oil.

Olive oil has been used in lamps in southern Europe since at least the time of the ancient Greeks.

The first oil well, Titusville, Pennsylvania

The first oil well was sunk in 1859. Soon paraffin was being distilled from crude oil and paraffin lamps became very popular. They were much brighter than previous lamps or candles, though they still used a wick.

For most of history the majority of poor families in Europe used reed lamps. Fuel for reed lamps was melted-down fat from meat, called tallow. The tallow would seep up a reed wick planted in it. When the tip of the reed was lit, the tallow burned slowly, giving light and a slight smell of food. Reed lamps are no longer used because of the smell, the poor light, and the bother of making tallow and wicks.

The Chinese were the first to use gas light. There are early Chinese references to bamboo pipes being filled with marsh gas (methane).

In a Tilly lamp, paraffin vapor burns brightly as it passes through a fine net structure called a mantle.

The fluorescent light is a glass tube coated on the inside with chemicals that glow, or fluoresce, when electricity is passed through a gas within the tube. Unlike other electric lights, fluorescent strips do not get hot and they give a bright economical light. Fluorescent lighting became known to the general public after the New York World's Fair in 1939.

Davy lamps were invented by Sir Humphrey Davy in 1815. A very explosive gas called methane, or fire damp, builds up in mines. It caused many disasters when lit by the naked candle flames carried by early miners. In Davy's lamp the flame is covered by a wire gauze with 120 holes per square centimeter, so methane cannot get through the gauze in enough quantity to explode. Instead, the flame becomes brighter when methane is present, warning the miner of possible danger.

Good candles were often more expensive than oil lamps. They were originally made from tallow and so were rather smelly, but were later made from beeswax or paraffin wax. They are still widely used because some people consider harsh electric light to be less attractive.

The wick on a candle has to be plaited so that it falls sideways and does not put out the flame.

WINDOWS

The trouble with houses is that if they have no holes in their walls they are dark, and if they do have holes in their walls they are either drafty or too hot. Windows help to solve this problem. A window is a hole in the wall, usually with a piece of transparent material placed across it, so that light can enter, but wind and rain are kept out.

Houses in hot countries have small windows to reduce the flow of hot air into the cool, shady interior.

In cooler countries, where light is needed but not the cold wind, small windows are built in the walls of houses where the coldest winds blow. Larger windows are built in the opposite walls to catch the heat of the sun.

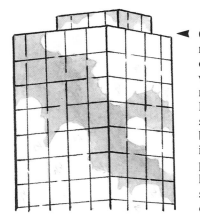

Outer skins of large, modern buildings are often "glass curtains" which may be tinted to reflect the sun's heat. Recently, glass with a special clear coating has been developed that lets in light and heat but prevents heat from leaving. This is useful for saving heating energy in cold countries.

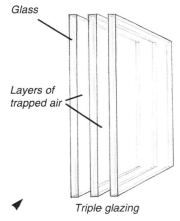

Glass

Layers of trapped air

Triple glazing

Air is a poor conductor of heat. A layer of air trapped between two sheets of glass reduces the amount of heat lost from a building, and also reduces noise. In some cold places, like Norway and Sweden, triple glazing is built into all new homes.

In the Arabian desert, the Bedu tribespeople roll up the sides of their tents to let in light and air.

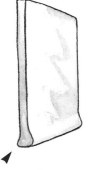

Glass actually acts like a very thick liquid. Over the years, glass sheets flow downwards so that they are thicker at the bottom than the top.

Japanese houses traditionally have no glass windows, possibly because Japan is in an earthquake zone. Instead sliding doors are covered with rice paper, which allows light to filter in.

Windows must provide security against intruders. The earliest windows were holes that could be closed with shutters.

The Romans used glass in their windows but they could not produce large, flat, clear pieces. Their glass windows were very small.

In the Middle Ages windows were often covered with a thin layer of horn, oilcloth, or waxed paper. Wooden shutters with decorative holes were also used.

In the fourteenth century, glass was spun from a large disk of molten glass which was flat around the edges but ridged like the bottom of a glass bottle in the center. Flat thick "crown" glass was cut from the edges, leaving "bottle" glass in the center, which was either recycled or used by someone who did not mind the distortion.

In Tudor cottages small diamonds of crown glass were joined together by lead strips. By 1918 larger pieces of plate glass were made by grinding and smoothing flat ribbons of molten glass drawn from a heating vat.

Float glass was introduced in 1952. Sheets of molten glass are floated on molten tin. The tin is smooth and flat, and glass does not stick to it. When the glass is cool enough and smooth on both sides it's taken off on rollers.

Sash windows slide up and down. The moving parts are balanced by counterweights set in the frame on each side of the window to make opening and closing the window easy. They were first used in the seventeenth century.

A casement window is hinged on one side and has a latch to hold it open or closed.

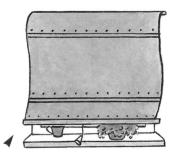

Roller blinds are space-saving, instant coverings for windows.

Venetian blinds are vertical or horizontal slats of wood, metal, or plastic that can be adjusted to let in varying amounts of light.

Net curtains make it difficult for passersby to see into houses during daylight hours.

ALL LOCKED UP

The design of both doors and locks has changed over the centuries, but not the reason why we need them. In some cases even the design remains the same — there is a lock in use in Egypt today based on a design which may be over three thousand years old.

Janus was the Roman god of doorways and of beginnings and endings. He had two faces and could look both forward and backward at the same time.

The Romans had folding doors that moved on pivots fixed into the sill and the lintel.

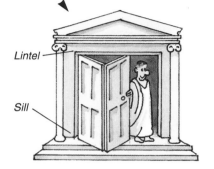

Lintel

Sill

The earliest examples of metal hinges are made of copper and were found on treasure chests in the tomb of the Pharaoh Tutankhamen (1357–1338 B.C.).

Roman coin showing Janus

This door hinge, first patented in 1799, lifts the door over the edge of a rug.

Knobs and latches

Standard round knob. Difficult for some people to turn.

This type is easy to turn but can catch on clothes.

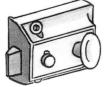

The Yale lock provides good security.

The Suffolk latch is used where security is unnecessary.

Wooden doors are heavy. They hang from the side and not from the top, so the door tends to get pulled out of shape by its own weight. Strong vertical and horizontal crosspieces reduce this distortion, and lighter inset panels reduce the overall weight.

Roman iron key

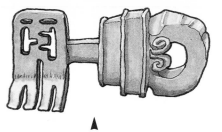

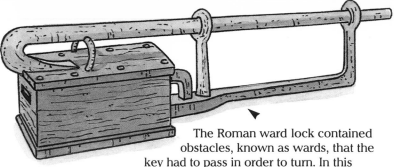

The first locks and keys were wooden and were probably invented by the Chinese about 4,500 years ago. The Romans developed complex iron and bronze locks.

The Roman ward lock contained obstacles, known as wards, that the key had to pass in order to turn. In this Romano-British lock the turning key moved a huge bolt.

Metal padlocks were first produced in Nuremberg in the 1540s, where they were used for locking boxes.

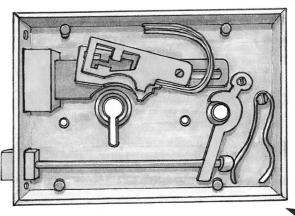

Edwardian mortise lock

In 1778 Robert Barron, an English locksmith, together with Joseph Bramah (see below) made the forerunner to the mortise lock. These use levers that must be moved an exact distance by the key before the bolt can be moved.

Joseph Bramah patented the first barrel lock in 1784. His key had slits and notches that depressed spring segments in a cylinder to different depths. At the correct depth the groove on the edge of all the segments lined up and the entire barrel could be revolved by the key to draw the bolt. Bramah was so confident of the security of his invention that he offered 200 guineas to anyone who could pick it. Sixty-seven years later, at the Great Exhibition of 1851, an American locksmith, Alfred Hobbs, succeeded, but only after hours of laborious effort.

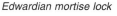

For most of history, people have kept their valuables in large heavy chests or strongboxes. The first secure, fireproof safe was introduced by Thomas Milner and Charles Chubb in 1845.

Most bank safes have a time lock so that the safe can be opened only at certain times.

The Yale lock, patented in 1865 by an American, Linus Yale, Jr., has been the most successful lock of all time. The five wards have an almost infinite variety of positions, so it is very secure.

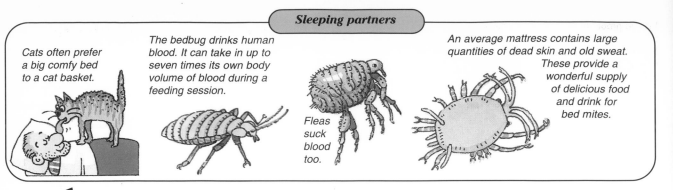

Cats often prefer a big comfy bed to a cat basket.

The bedbug drinks human blood. It can take in up to seven times its own body volume of blood during a feeding session.

Fleas suck blood too.

An average mattress contains large quantities of dead skin and old sweat. These provide a wonderful supply of delicious food and drink for bed mites.

AND SO TO BED

We spend about a third of our lives in bed so it's important to be comfortable and warm. In the past, people often shared their beds with the rest of the family, especially on cold nights. Even farm animals sometimes slept in the same room!

Headboards prevent pillows from falling off the end of the bed. Footboards prevent bedclothes from falling ▲ off the other end.

▲ The Indian charpoy is a simple wooden bedstead with netting for support.

▲ South American Indians and Caribs slept in hammocks made of woven material. The idea was adopted by Europeans for their ships because hammocks allow sleeping sailors to remain undisturbed by the rolling of the ship.

The Celestial Bed was invented by Dr. James Graham in about 1778. It was surrounded by 1,680 pounds (762 kg) of magnets, which he claimed were good for the health. There was a charge of 500 gold coins a night to sleep in it.

High-sided bunk beds on ships helped to prevent passengers and sailors from falling out during stormy weather.

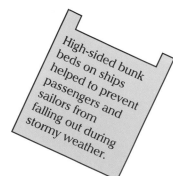

The Japanese futon is a slatted wooden bed that is usually covered with a cotton-padded mattress.

Camp-beds were first used by soldiers when on campaign. Officers took collapsible beds with them. The Egyptian Pharaoh Tutankhamen used a fold-up bed when traveling around his kingdom.

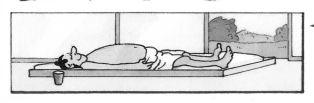

You've probably met smarty-pants people who think they are always right – but hardly ever are! Take Know-it-all Ned for example. Most of what he's saying is rubbish! Can you tell when he's right and when he's wrong?

KNOW-IT-ALL NED'S

QUIZ

"...the baseball bat is rounded because early baseball grew out of a game in which the round handle of a cricket bat was used to hit a ball..."

"Samovars are special teapots named after an Irish explorer who introduced tea into Europe in 1536..."

"...some Indians hang up wet grass to cool their houses..."

"...Roman generals used strops to protect their feet against hypocausts..."

"...modern fountain pens were invented by Mr. Waterman in 1884..."

"...ward locks are so named because they help to prevent burglaries in hospitals..."

"...olive oil was used in lamps by ancient southern Europeans..."

"...medieval monks recycled scrolls for toilet paper..."

"...dried cow dung is used for cooking food in some countries in Asia and Africa."

"...float glass is called this after the process by which it is made..."

"...frozen fish was first eaten by a shipwrecked sailor, Finlay Codburger, in 1868..."

"...in the game of Ching, Chang, Pok, runny noses can be covered by hankies..."

ANSWERS

1: Wrong (see page 7)
2: Wrong (p. 2, p. 21)
3: Right (p. 21)
4: Wrong (p. 18)
5: Right (p. 25)
6: Wrong (p. 29)
7: Wrong (p. 3)
8: Right (p. 15)
9: Right (p. 27)
10: Wrong (p. 5)
11: Right (p. 4)
12: Wrong (p. 9)

31

INDEX

First American Edition 1996 by
Franklin Watts
A Division of Grolier Publishing
Sherman Turnpike
Danbury, Connecticut 06816

© 1996 Lazy Summer Books Ltd
Illustrated by Lazy Summer Books Ltd
Printed in Belgium

Wilcox, Jane.
    Why do we use that? / by Jane Wilcox.
        p. cm. — (Why do we?)
    Includes index.
    Summary: Describes a variety of inventions
in such categories as toys and games, home
entertainment, and sports.
    ISBN 0-531-14395-3 (lib. bdg.)
    1. Inventions — Juvenile literature
[1. Inventions.] I. Title. II. Series.
T48.W54 1996   95–38264
603.8'09 — dc20   CIP
                                        AC